Advance Praise for *Remembering the Truth*

"Janice Krasselt Tatter's collection of poetry, *Remembering the Truth,* is filled with haunting honesty. Without using scorn, self-pity, or judgment, she portrays her memories with vivid images that leave the reader with a sense of raw immediacy.

This is a brave book that addresses the power of intimacy and memory. Janice writes of subjects we all know- food, photos, vacations, neighbors, and then finds a way to make us feel as if we haven't really known these things because she travels so deeply to show us that meal, that image, that beach, those people next door. These poems are a journey of experiences that add a new dimension to one's daily existence."

--Diane Payne, author of *Burning Tulips*

Remembering the Truth

Poems by Janice Krasselt Tatter

Temenos Publishing ~ Little Rock, AR

Remembering the Truth
Copyright © 2006 by Janice Krasselt Tatter
All rights reserved

ISBN 0-9785648-1-2

Cover Art by Mitchell Crisp Patterson

Temenos Publishing • 303 Rice St. • Little Rock, AR 72205 •
USA • 501-920-7803
www.temenospublishing.com

ACKNOWLEDGMENTS

Grateful acknowledgment is made to the following publications where these poems or earlier versions of them first appeared:

Passport Journal: "Obsessions"
Poesia: "Being Noticed"
              "A Phantom Perspective"
              "Afterwards"
Poetry Motel: "The Ritual"
Southern Hum: "Recipes"
              "Black Onyx"
              "Record Heat"

Many thanks to Paula Morell, David Jauss, Linda VanBlaricom, Nikki Wright, Tim Muren, Roberta Kroll, Alanis Morisssette, and my classmates at A Way With Words Writing Workshops.

To the memory of my parents who always believed.

CONTENTS

I.

III.

I.

The search for truth is more precious than its possession.

--Albert Einstein

RECIPES

My husband and I exchange acidic words,
then decide not to speak. We listen only
to the sounds of the new neighbors next door.
They don't know we can hear every word.
They don't know we can hear cries
in sex, body rumbles, the abrupt silence
afterwards that filters into our sparse rooms
and makes me blush.

Inside the apartment
it's difficult for me to imagine her
in clothes. I picture her voluptuous,
shrugging off her nine-to-five suit,
floating nude through her own rooms,
painting lavender oil words
on her husband's back. They hold each other,
any pain between them dissolving
into loving gestures, her hand on his chest,
his finger on her cheek. He feeds her grapes
at every meal, each one held higher and higher
until her back arches, the bite
slow as she closes her mouth
over the fruit. She offers him
strawberries, spoonfuls of lemon sorbet.

I recognize their voices at the grocery.
She and her husband both husky, gray hair,

flannel shirts, turn from each other
indifferent, carry bread, potatoes, onions.
I want them to buy arugula, basil,
red snapper filets, Merlot, cream,
debate flat-leaf versus curly parsley,
hold hands as they shop.

I want to tell them through thin insulation
how because of them we've begun
to whisper, make love in murmurs,
hold each other again, that tonight
we'll have pork medallions, wild rice,
cranberry chutney, pears poached in wine.

RECORD HEAT

1.
I return to the duplex
where we lived upstairs,
where I learned heat rises.
Below is plump Anne,
my age of seven.
She shows me her half house,
cooler than mine,
the tang of urine everywhere,
her brother the teenaged bed wetter,
everyday his half sheet hanging
on the clothesline,
the Virgin Mary, crucifixes
on mantles and walls,
the black piano no one plays,
glistening in that smell of urine.
I used to think
I was in a museum
of things untouched,
of things once believed.

2.
I pulled peaches from the fridge
and held them close to my cheeks,
pretending peach-rose rouge,
then under my shirt, delighted
in my sudden womanly blossoms.

3.

On the news a rainmaker whose potion
makes rain clouds in five days.
Only children believed in his downpours.
Across the city men took bets,
the odds unlikely.
But it was better than nothing,
better than living. And so this man
no one knew cast his chemical spell to the sky
and in five days it rained
for a few minutes, enough to win bets,
but not enough for relief when the heat
returned to take our breath again.

4.

We moved to keep cool that summer—
movies, lakes, long country drives,
trips to rows of shops downtown,
any place with air conditioning or wind,
even on Sundays, once reserved only for church.
Donna Reed wore gloves and hats and pearls
and people died sleeping on blocks of ice.

THE DAY LULLS IN ANESTHESIA

1.

After migraines in that marriage years ago,
I used to long for days like these.
I remember our return to Oxford,
where we celebrated centuries,
bypassed the present on High Street.
Cold that summer, we bought heavy sweaters,
cough syrup, dressed in shivers by light
of gas stove. At night, port and cigars
in tuxedos at St. John's. I had
a migraine, the reason for my absence
at High Table, cured by hours of sleep
and sherry. I dreamed I awoke
and you were there, stroking my head,
pulling me around you like a new day.

2.

Like lovers in a musical, we'll embrace
the distant thunder, the afternoon
shower. We'll tap dance in rain
to Cole Porter, my dress in whirls
of lilac. We'll sing in harmony
from treetop to treetop, our voices proclaiming
fathoms of love. I dismiss another migraine.

Imagine the music in our life.

3.

No. There was never pretense.
How I feared new days, the prospect
of pain, that you might not be there
for the here and now of the migraine—
the comforter heavy, the down pillow
hard, I see yellow lights change to white knives
like a murderer piercing everything in his sight,
the eye, the brain, the flesh
in rhythms of flashing neon lights,
skin clammy, hands shaking, face pale
as winter, the clock movements
too slow or too fast like a bad dream
where legs move in quicksand
or race endless in streams of naked gauntlets.
The pain wins and I vomit
again and again. I remember fear
the way I remember migraines,
the half vision, the selfish pain
aching for more.

LAST RITE

His hands go up for prayer.
The priest anoints him
with oil, the sign
of the cross made with thumb
on forehead. My father
lies gaunt, his collarbone thick
and protruding, his chest
sunken over paper-thinned skin, prominent ribs.
When the priest whispers
into his ear, my father murmurs back,
his cheeks wet. He tells me
he can taste his tears.

He lost partial hearing in Korea.
I was never certain how much
he heard. I had to repeat
every word, write long letters.
Now with the priest,
he can hear. After all these years,
I didn't know what to say.

Months ago my father told me
he dreamed Viet Cong,
how he knew he beat cancer
when he killed the last VC,
a man whose shadow

cursed and mocked him,
evaded sight, the light of day.

Go back to Carlsbad Caverns,
before cancer cells invaded,
before my brother, before Vietnam.
I am nine. I smell the damp cold
in the cave dense with darkness,
startled bats. As I hear

my words echo
for the first time
like a litany in a hushed church,
my hands go up for prayer.
My father holds me tight.

CHILD

Could be, maybe, might have been, never was
are words that describe my child.
Over years he has grown from his imaginative life
into my days and is as vivid to me now
as his reluctant father—20 now,
short, dark, intense, intelligent.
I tell him over and over how I wanted
to be his mother, how I grieve
his might have been, never was life,
never becoming more than one cell, never growing
his spirit into toes, fingers, heart, brain on a sonogram,
never finding himself in my arms, on my breasts.
I've actually named him.
And where is he when he's not with me?
Was my David promised to another?
I look into brown eyes of 20-year-olds
and wonder sometimes
if he might recognize the one-half
who wanted to create him.

THIRTEEN

Every summer Brent and I
would bicycle to the city pool,
our diving masks strapped to our heads.
For hours, we'd dive for pennies on the bottom
of the three-foot water section,
intent on being the one to collect
the most coins. One day
my swimsuit strap
slipped off my shoulders
leaving one small breast exposed.
Brent's face never changed
but suddenly we stopped diving
and on the ride home that day
he let me ride in front,
opened my screen door.
When he put his arm around my shoulders,
the way he'd done a thousand times,
his skin was cool, moist.
I remember wanting to hold his hand,
reassure him, my heart burning
with fear, my hand reaching up instead
to smooth back my wind-blown hair.

BEING NOTICED

I remember sitting on a stool in a drugstore
wanting to buy a Coke. I didn't know how
to get the waitress' attention
so I kept turning around and around
in my tall, red seat, squeezing my three nickels
in my sweaty palm. The huge counter,
its edge above my head,
the waitress who peered over everyone,
the man on my right in a gray suit
who glared at me as my arm brushed his,
the man on my left with greased-back hair
and a leather jacket whose fingers
tapped his glass and as I kept turning,
he began to watch my feet.
Finally I released the coins,
the nickels falling on the counter,
spinning before resting flat.
"I have money," I announced.

AFTERWARDS

You wash dishes.
I come from behind,
my arms around your waist,
a gesture so simple
I don't think about it
until you freeze,
and we are in that moment,
the plate in mid-air
between cleaned and rinsed,
the water running.
You tell me
only one thing at a time
and I pull back,
dry the plate in silence,
my reflection
a new light in the kitchen.

THE RITUAL

A friend and her husband, a mortician,
live above the embalming room in a funeral home.
With her hands fanning the air, she describes
how their rooms fill with the scent of roses,
sometimes the organ's somber hum. Nights
when her husband embalms, she can't sleep
for the noises below--the table creaking
as he adjusts its height, the whir
from machines doing things she suspects,
but doesn't want explained. Before coming
back to bed, he takes long showers. Afterwards
once she saw him scrub his clean hands
over and over at the sink. She says
she'll never forget his quiet way
of lying next to her, hearing him breathe
warm air into his hands before turning
to stroke her shoulders.

II.

If you do not tell the truth about yourself, you can't tell it about
other people.

--Virginia Woolf

BLACK ONYX
(after Leslie Ullman)

This stone is the color of discord,
the color of that marriage in another century,
where we lived in a cottage surrounded
by oak trees, each room so small and dark
I called the place a treehouse
and became claustrophobic.
We drifted to company dinners
where we toasted others
with one glass of Chablis after another.
I had migraines so severe
I saw only half of my married life.
I wore long, colorful skirts
and ate no meat.
I sautéed tofu
coated in black sesame seeds,
garnished with cilantro.
My husband never noticed
I painted my nails clear
and wore Swiss watches.
He never noticed when nervous
I'd finger a black onyx ring
I bought myself one anniversary.
My husband smoked cigars
and there were always words
like his curls of smoke whiffling
between us hinting disaster

and one year for Lent
I fasted during the day,
gave up speaking to him.
My silence persisted beyond forty days
but I never felt cleansed. Inside
I was screaming.
That's how we stopped listening,
our words growing shorter and shorter
until we said nothing.

HANDICAP

My mother started to cook
when she became a widow.
She loved to make tuna salad with diced apples,
bacon and asparagus on toast with lumpy cheese sauce.
She used regular teaspoons to measure
and the seasoning was either too much
or too little. Always
in pain, she sat on a stool to cook,
her right leg shorter than the left,
a built-up shoe of three inches
that cost $200. I knew
no one had a mother more beautiful.
She wore slacks to cover scars on the right leg,
her hands long and colorful,
coral nails and large, oval stones
on fingers gnarled by arthritis.
I felt plain by comparison. I felt
protective, especially when strangers
stared at her shoe. Because of her, I noticed
too-low seats in homes and doctors' offices,
heights of stairs, degrees of inclines,
distances from curb to doors,
frankness of children, fear of a snowfall,
pain in walking.

LIKE BESSIE SMITH: THE SECOND NOTE LOUNGE

When Vera's favorite singer, Bessie,
bled to death in that car crash in Mississippi,
Vera stopped singing. In tribute to Bessie,

she orders martinis extra dry. She likes anything
straight up. Men who fill
the smoky bar visit this woman none

would marry. For moments her past is forgiven.
She slips the fox stole off her shoulder,
hums men to chairs beside her. Martini extra dry.

She rolls an olive in her mouth before turning
to men. One man's hand touches her thigh
like Bessie Smith's voice seeping wet.

He's a cop always coming for her dissonance.
This woman Vera will let men do anything at the bar
if she can get a drink. Sometimes the music starts

when she arrives every night in the same stole,
or if she crescendos by herself.
Early nights her hand shakes, the glass unwilling

to hide her tremors. *Martini, sir, hold the olive*
orders a blond man behind her. She guides his hand
down onto her right breast and turns her face

as oboes squeal. This time he's so close
he can lick her martini. They are not done.
He asks for another drink and she accepts,

leans backward so he feels both breasts.
She speaks only with her body. His hand trembles
rough inside her dress. His voice changes deep.

Please, baby. Let's leave. The music murmurs.
She is *glissando*, he *allegro*, then *appassionata*.
She holds up her glass in a thank you, turns away.

It's her game-- Martini. Fondling. Martini.
He refuses to give up, tugs at her dress, the black
and white lilies now cuttings, her breasts

bare. A knife appears, the steel tip bloody
after she cuts his hand. He pulls torn
lilies as he reaches for her breasts. She screams

you fucker bastard and slashes his cheek.
You're lucky I didn't slice your dick off she yells
as he crawls away. She wraps her stole around her bodice,

moves to a side chair. As the bar empties,
the piano player remains. The bartender
whispers to her *your music moves me so.*

He sits beside her, the blood fallen notes on the floor.
He fills her glass, runs his hand up her dress,
kisses her cheek as he feels her come quickly.

An olive rolls in her mouth, and she hums low,
so only he can hear Bessie's song
"A Good Man is Hard to Find."

A HISTORY OF ROSES
(after Leslie Ullman)

My hands suddenly resemble my mother's,
her hands like her mother's,
her hands her mother's,

and on and on
until I'm dizzy counting backwards.
My hands are not my own.

Perhaps my body I thought
I owned is not mine. Perhaps
everything is an illusion.

My hands float in dreams.
I count fingers
belonging to someone else.

I hold roses with fingers
stained bloody on thorns.
Fanning the air, I smell

roses filling each room,
where lovers leave at dawn,
their beds with virgin blood,

rose petals over clothes
hastily abandoned in piles,

fingers finding themselves

on masculine faces
stroke open eyes, mouths,
touching tongues like kisses,

caressing hidden parts.
I write love letters with quills.
In return a man calls

at the door. My head bends to roses
he brought me. I finger rosary beads,
sign the cross on my forehead and chest.

My fingers touch a baby's face,
my hands cupping my breast
into an infant's mouth, its shape

like a rose opening for sun.
My fingers trace weddings, births,
baptisms, deaths in the Bible.

When I turn its pages
pressed roses fall out.
My hands suddenly cover my eyes

for lost generations—
I wail over open coffins of twin girls,

the mother who died in childbirth,

the banished woman who loved an Englishman.
As red calloused hands pour tea,
the tea leaves hint strong, superstitious women.

When I wake up,
my hands begin to whisper Gaelic,
hold themselves in a light

stilled from dawn, the scent
of dried roses in steamer trunks,
the floral leaves that set on dancing heads

when days were never counted.

A PHANTOM PERSPECTIVE

Imagine a sleepless life
without dreams and no need
for night. Lovers would never know
moonlight walks,
clinging to each other
in the cold dark, the smell of grass
under starry heavens, the sounds—
cricket, owls,
yowling coyotes, and cats.
The sun would never rise nor set.
We'd know darkness only
when we chased our shadows
and closed our eyes to blink.

REMEMBERING THE TRUTH

The last time we had sex—
I say sex, not made love,
because you admitted
the love was gone
or did we agree
it was never there?—
I cried after you entered me
and for those moments
I remembered
or thought I remembered
the history of our passion
or was it always pure lust?
So much has happened
I can't keep things straight.
I remember clearly now—
I cried and you came in silence.
I took a short bath.
Now I remember
I made love while you had sex.
That's how it was.
How could I have forgotten?

THE VACANT LOT

The light dulls the day as morning closes cold.
Shadows flicker. I embrace this slow beginning
of a day with coffee. Gradually the afternoon opens.
I walk to a vacant lot. Old tires swinging on an oak
could be men dangling from their necks,
their feet high above the ground,
swaying in wind, bodies heavy, elusive.
An oil drum rusted and filled with ashes
rests on its side. I see condoms,
broken bottles scattered.
In another life I'd walk away,
taking time only to shiver, shake off
the distaste. Now I discover
my own likeness in a broken mirror
discarded in the oil drum. I touch it,
slivers of glass cutting my finger,
the blood pooling in ashes below like pieces
of myself I don't want to recognize.
I should be more careful.

WEDDING ALBUM

In this wedding picture, I bend to yellow roses,
baby breath like delicate wishes
woven throughout the bouquet.
I'm captured forever smiling
as only cameras can show.
Other pictures from several albums—
my mother kissing me at Christmas,
my husband in scuba gear,
our anniversary champagne toasts
in fluted glasses hoisted in the air of good wishes,
each year the smiles weaker, glasses
held lower, vacations in Oxford and Florence,
where we surrounded ourselves with students,
their smiles our substitutes, the vacation in Destin
when our eyes began to open.
Absent from cameras are days we only mumbled
our separate agendas, his panic
of possible pregnancy, the silence
in our lives like blisters. Some eight years later
I received the divorce papers.
I don't have a picture
of the nausea, my unsteady hands.
But in that last picture I have of him,
the day we separated,
he's reading the newspaper. I had never
seen him so sad. I'm adding
this picture to the wedding album.

HORSEPLAY

Classmates giggle boys,
she sounds whinnies.
Her legs delicate spindles,
she canters in circles
around the playground.
Her long hair, now tail,
flicks away flies,
a gentle unassuming motion
so natural we begin to believe.
Each day her face grows long as dreams,
her nostrils breathe memories,
the eyes gleam stone
touched by lava.
Standing up she sleeps hard,
that tail flicking ever so often
and when she awakes morning,
her muscles grow as powerful as words
we feed her—*beautiful, magnificent.*
When she abandons us
for fields of clover, she reveals
haunting memories have taken her
to times when skies have become horizons,
to times of caves, before words.
I could live forever like this, she says.

A LINEAR PERSPECTIVE

Today is Tuesday, and we're here in photos
drunk on sun at Destin's packed beach.
I remember the first day how you arose
from water, a masked man who breeds
duplicity. Trudging deep in sand,
you show me your net of shells, ignoring
the curious around me like they were the predators.
I murmur shyness, other excuses
I had memorized for years
when your eyes dilate dark silences.
I marked this day as indifference
and I moved forward
as if the future meant beginnings.

That night you hunt sandcrabs darting
from flashlights. In this too dark photo,
one as big as a thumb eats insects.
I discover sand dollars in broken pieces.
I tell you how sad it is that no one
cares for these shell fragments abandoned
on the shoreline. Only you know
how I have pieced segments together
like torn valentines and framed them
in white sand too bright in sun.

Here's your favorite.
You are mask and fins, your red flag posted deep.

This photo hangs in your office beside starfish,
sand dollars. I see sea oats
straining in Gulf breezes as nothing
went right that day. We missed the sunrise
cruise. I chased our beach umbrella
needlessly in wind. You went diving,
your net empty as you returned. You told me
algae are moving in, that you had seen sting rays
big as your torso and maybe a small shark,
how you wished I wasn't so scared of emerald water
or the unforeseen. You went back to swim,
and I heard you cursing the day.

Our last night we watched fishing boats
slip away in a moonlight and a clarity we had never found
hunting sandcrabs at midnight, on the river Thames or Seine,
or in any place in our life. We tiptoe
into the water's edge, surprisingly cold,
full of algae.

We never ventured any farther.

BREAST SURGEON

Drama alone could kill in this office.
The staff alone hold my wet hand
in every conversation. I wish
for a lazy nurse of sarcastic body language
so I could complain—
boxes of tissues align exactly on tabletops,
paired clownfish bob in the aquarium,
celery and lavender women of somber lithographs,
pink scrubs, soft, low voices,
always end in lilting questions.
I prefer back and white...period.
I wait for the doctor, convinced
the thick air here doubts survival.

BOSTON, 1966

After a year's duty in Vietnam, my father
returned to the States to notify
surviving kin of dead or missing soldiers.
In his dress blues, he'd appear on doorsteps,
his presence enough to make fathers cry,
mothers wail on the floor before he said a word.
He'd always clear his throat.
"I'm sorry," he'd say,
and they'd shake their fists or heads.

There were no flags waving,
no ribbons around trees,
no stars in windows,
no neighbor to rush over,
and more than once
he saw a father spit on the flag
folded in that puffed triangle presented
by the honor guard.

Some mothers and fathers wanted to talk.
What had he seen in the war?
He told them the only story I heard,
how he'd seen a village of women
and children gunned down by the Viet Cong,
their decayed bodies piled high
as bamboo trees. The children looked
especially fearful, their hands stiff curls

as if grasping dreams of escape. Mothers
cradled babies' heads and pushed them
toward their breasts, how this position
gave the VC a perfect shot
at the backs of heads. My father
cried every time he told this part.

SIX DEGREES

Faucets drip all over town,
plants are draped in burlap, animals
murmur inside.
A bank sign sputters 6 degrees.
He looks Indian, a scarf twisted
around ears and head like a turban,
a long Army coat soiled from weeks
of booze, vomit of hangovers, nosebleeds
from scuffles. His feet are heavy with cold.
No outstretched palms tonight.
In the distance he hears the incantation
of alley voices, men haggling over a joint
as rats scurry inside a vacant landing.
He eludes cop cars like shelters
full of warm lice, stands by a fire.

He remembers stories of hopping the rails,
The C&I, Missouri Pacific, trestles
over mountains and rivers, the whistle-stop towns
whose names arose like oases in flat lands,
Sweet Home, Delight, Star City,
their houses marked
for quick food and work. Hobos.
A good life compared to this
begging for money, now
a sophomoric scavenger hunt. Might as well
be dead on a dead night, the sky giving up

its heat and light so selfishly. He curses
these cold days. When the fire dies out,
all he can do is walk a little faster.

BE STILL, MY HEART

I never imagined my first serenade,
the sudden moon rising deliberate
over us, crickets and honeysuckle
my only witnesses.
I was amused at first
then quite flattered
when I realized he'd ridden miles,
the guitar strapped to his bike.
I didn't know this bearded man
would change my life forever
as he opened his mouth, played
the refrain on his guitar
like some Don Juan.
There were no bells, no intervention
by my heart putting me on alert
to this moment in the making.
I didn't know the song,
something about young love,
but I was certain about the way
he sang, the way he touched
my face before kissing me.

III.

The truth may hurt but a lie can cut a deeper wound.

--Unknown

REPAIRS

As a young rider, that black gelding
clearing a three-foot fence
by six feet scared me
into thinking death.
How I wanted to ride at a fox hunt in pinks
with coupled fox hounds, jumping
with ease over stone fences in England.
Braiding his mane and tail
to protect him from mud was easier than
shielding him from Arkansas sun
to keep him from turning brown.
At his withers fifteen hands,
his black mouth met my hands exactly
for carrots every evening when I later
dreamed myself over every fence I could imagine—
that feeling of being one in air
as we swelled together for moments
defying gravity, peeling back
layers to feel that part of my self.
Still today I go back to that piece of me
galloping farther each time
across straw-dried fields, higher fences,
across time, across wounds long abandoned,
filling those holes until once again,
I ride childlike, whole.

ARIA

She thought she loved him.
After all wasn't he the one
she talked to endlessly nights
and into mornings? Wasn't he
the one who listened, actually listened?
Didn't he whisper her name over and over
when they made love? And when she couldn't sleep
didn't he hum her favorite tune?
He was there in the room so close
he could wipe her tears. The mirror's
reflection shows them holding hands.
She reaches up, kisses him
full on the mouth. He walks away,
the room now blurred as outside
fog settles over the valley
and lurks like thin clouds of music.
What comes between them
will transform their lives,
their harmony together.
See how she hurries after him,
his sorrow of failed notes
rising in solitude. Nothing
else matters. She thought
she loved him. She thought
he loved her.

BEGINNINGS

Start with a wheel,
fire in a wheatfield,
the long blade made from flint.
We eat dandelion greens,
sip rainwater from our hands,
draw pictures in dirt, sleep
like children deep in the woods.
We marvel at rainbows, sculpted
muscles of a horse, the way we feel
touching each other. Climbing trees,
we tremble at heights.
We know no better.
For all we know the purpose
is simply to be, to repeat what we've seen. Every day
we watch our shadows,
certain that memory saves us
from ourselves.

THE CAPTIVE

August. My fever of 102 degrees
is equal to the temperature outside.
I'm under three blankets
shivering. There's no one
here. I'm talking to the walls.
There's a mockingbird outside my window
who won't keep quiet. It's as if
he's singing only to me
and he goes on and on
without end. If I could get out of bed,
I'd try to kill him…at least
throw a shoe, something to stop his noise.
I swear he knows I'm helpless.
He's relentless in his longing to be heard.
I'm his captive and I don't want
to hear his song. Sometimes
I simply want to be alone.

DESTIN

We drink Taddy Porter
and toast the sun, this white beach
on our first trip to Destin,
discuss the heroes in a novel
we read out loud, and gradually
over the week I become
someone else to you, the heroine
who fears nothing, not even fantasies—
we ride waves on a board,
swim with dolphins
at the aquarium, make love
every sunrise and sunset,
drift in shadows of the water's surface,
then immerse ourselves in vivid blues and whites
of Destin's godly design.
I tell you I want the Gulf to become
a measure of our life—deep and expansive
without riptides, sharks, and algae. You hold me tight
and I reassure you that in these seven days,
I feel reborn, baptized in sun and sand.
I return to the novel, to the part
where the heroine remains strong, loving.

WILD FLOWERS

No one knew we were a couple,
the wild flowers just a ruse,
opening on my desk like afterthoughts
gathered by my apartment,
the picnic by the train tracks.
We talked incessantly in private,
every thought spilling out—
there was so much to learn,
our heaving bodies so thirsty
we became one,
and we sighed in amazement
at how we could find each other
in unison, our muscles glistening
in sweaty pleasure,
the words on our lips
reduced to pure breath.

THE NEIGHBORHOOD

My neighborhood has preserved its small gabled houses
sprawling on lots between gingko trees and weeping willows.
In autumn, the gingko leaves,

a shade brighter than mustard, spread themselves
on the ground in perfect patterns of a round quilt.
Every day my elderly neighbors rake and rake

slowly, methodically, as if time were a fable.
On weekends, holidays, great-grandchildren sing
in leaf piles, shriek from hammocks, their welcomed

voices vanishing late Sundays when the still air
of other eras returns once again to empty trees.
Sometimes there's the smell of burning leaves.

At the supermarket, these same neighbors in their seventies,
eighties push carts with the same methodical dignity
they rake leaves. Stopping to visit, one couple chats

with another while lines on both aisles grow long as years.
I'm the only shopper who seems to mind, the only restless
soul in the store who pleads with clocks. One woman

stooped at the waist cannot read the price of oatmeal, asks
to borrow my eyes. Two aisles over, I'm trapped
between two women who debate the shape of grapefruit

for three minutes before deciding on Ruby Reds. I'm learning
decisions may last a lifetime. At the checkout,
a woman cannot find her money. With white hair,

large knuckles on hands like twigs, she leans on her cane,
murmuring, searching. Suddenly she produces coins
in handfuls. The eyes of the checker count the pile

of silver, his body restless behind his island. After she pays,
the elderly woman tells the checker he resembles
her grandson, produces pictures of auburn hair and freckles

flashing through leaves of plastic. Everyone in line admires
the handsome boy. I try to understand the long line is merely
a rehearsal of things to come, a time when everything matters.

YEARLY VISIT

I remember my mother's laughter
on the phone, TV noise,
the dogs barking, her cigarette smoke
curling around her hands
in the air as she talked. It was never
quiet in the house and my husband
never adapted. He'd retreat
to the bedroom, announce
he was going to a motel
to get away from the dogs,
the smoke. I don't know why
I never let him leave
but I'd beg
and he'd stay, our visits always
stained by his silences, his brooding eyes.
What I remember most
is how my mother would interrupt
to talk to TV as if we were absent,
as if our words meant nothing.

ALANIS MORISSETTE SINGS JAGGED LITTLE PILL

My music had always been heavy rhythms,
simple rhymes. Between ordinary men
Mick Jagger or Steven Tyler appeared,
their mouths loud, raw,
their tongues full lust.
Their hands guided my hips to pleasure.
We'd come within moments.

One night on TV
I heard a woman all hair and leather.
Her hands, mouth cupped the mic
like a man she loved. Her music
infectious, orgasmic anger
in ghostly echoes. I didn't understand
how she knew me. We'd never met.

She has since moved onto my walls,
her music throughout the house.
Her words like no one's reflection,
I have swallowed them whole
again and again.

THE BOYFRIEND

She always defended him, even after he broke her glasses while she was wearing them. I looked past the bruises, her stooped back, the pain in her foot. I thought her cane was mere drama and all those pills she took I simply explained away. I never believed she was that damaged. Who could live in such confusion or rather who would live in such confusion?

She always defended him, even after she rolled down a flight of stairs. She's clumsy, he said, the kind who can't walk and talk at the same time, and the kind who expects a bushel of roses for every angry word.

She always defended him, even from her hospital bed when the police were notified. He hovered over her like a brother, holding her hand and wiping blood from her face. She was usually quiet when he was present, but this time she murmured thank you in a soft voice, the kind of voice one expects to hear in a hospital, hushed and full of reverence for the sick. From now on, he says, I'll watch her more closely.

OBSESSIONS

I became obsessed with weather
after Mary Gwen explained
how clouds, low streaks of silver,
high white tops, or any cloud,
it didn't matter, could turn into funnels,
angry spirals that suck up
houses, cars, people,
and this was how her grandparents died.
Every day was the same—
we'd pray for cloudless days,
then look at the sky.
If it was cloudy, we'd hover in corners,
our wet palms over our eyes.
We'd play outside only if the sky
was a perfect blue, the color of denim.
When I suddenly began to refold newspapers,
align each page, every section,
matching the edges exactly together,
the print made my hand black
as I smoothed out each page
like I was erasing the clouds outside
and for moments
the fear, the uncertainty.

FLORENCE

On the Arno River, I close my eyes
and hear the cadence of Italian,
connected to the terra cotta horizon,
the dying sun of painters' patterns,
even the stare of Mediterranean men.

Firenze is Italian for Florence
where gypsies drape sleeping bambinos
across their laps, mouths silent
as hands open like bowls for lire.
Beyond the Duomo, as surprising as one layer
of uncolored stone, natives speaking
with their hands push tourists out of queues,
shove past them in flocked plazas.
Concealing lire in shoes and brassiere,
I carry no purse. When someone touches my arm
at Santa Croce, I recoil like prey.
Here I trust no one,
not even priests absolving sins
with their blessings, the signs of the cross
vanishing into air.

This city shrouds everything I once believed.
I try to remember things as they were—
the friend who played Bach
as she died, her face powder white,
the eyes so fixed and calm

Rossetti would have painted the scene.
No.
The friend was a professor whose blood
covered volumes of books, that gun
his sole judge. The only sound he heard
was the morbid thud as a bullet lodged
before exploding in the brain.

I welcome the interruption at 3 a.m.
A woman below my hotel window
cannot find the door to the Hotel Porta Rossa.
She serpentines the cobblestones, her arm
outstretched like a lover on stage
imploring forgiveness. I close my eyes,
see the Arno River, hear the cadence of Italian.
This time the woman below curses
in American, her outstretched arm
holds Chianti. Though I yearn to watch
her tango with the polizia
who take her away, she staggers,
then withers in their arms.

BRUISES

The first time his thin hands groped
for her throat, his eyes narrowed
like dried vines and she remembered
the rustle of sheets
quietened with the dampness
their bodies created. The second time
she remembered her mother
mute when Father ran away that summer
when moonvine choked itself and smoldered
on the trellis.

In mirrors she palpates the yellowed bruises
like pulses. The strange marks still
so deep she could almost see his thumb
print, the circular maze
like a weather map of lows
and highs. In every room's mirror
she touches her neck and by day's end
she's memorized the splotches
as if they were beauty marks.

She smells moonvine in bloom, the trellis white
with blossoms, feels the leathered lines
of father's face or was it his hands, hears
her mother's nightly moaning like pasture sounds
of the mare bred in hobbles. No.
Father said it was house noises or boards,

the stallion wanting the mare. Touching
her neck, she hears that moaning,
her father's voice.

ABOUT THE AUTHOR

Janice Krasselt Tatter graduated with a B.A. from University of Arkansas at Little Rock in 1982. She graduated with an M.A. in English from Ohio University in 1984. Also an R.N., she held a variety of jobs after the M.A: college English instructor, grants proposal writer, and medical analyst for an insurance company. She wrote poetry intermittently until 2003 when she began to write full time. She is recipient of the Alma K. Daughtery Literary Award. Now in early retirement, she lives in Little Rock, Arkansas with her Boston Terrier, Buster.